REA

Smart Business Travel:

How to Stay Safe When You're on the Road

Stacey Ravel Abarbanel

First Books

Copyright © 1994 by First Books, Inc.

First Books, Inc. is not legally responsible for any change in the value of any enterprises by reasons of their inclusion or exclusion from this work. Contents are based on information believed to be accurate at the time of publication.

First Books, Inc., has not accepted payment from any firms or organizations for inclusion in this book.

Author: Stacey Ravel Abarbanel
Publisher: Jeremy Solomon
Copy Editor: Frieda Landau
Cover: Miles DeCoster
Interior: Gale DeCoster
Production: Special Projects
Contributors: Gail Miller, Leslie Morgan, Jodi Peterson

ISBN 0-912301-23-6

Manufactured in the United States of America by Versa Press, East Peoria, Illinois.

Published by First Books, Inc.
P.O. Box 578147, Chicago, IL 60657

TABLE OF CONTENTS

Introduction

The intent of this book is *not* to scare people. The fact is that executives are traveling more and more for business in an increasingly unsafe world, and this book offers some no-nonsense tips that can make your business travels more secure and relaxing.

Think for a moment about the many precautions you take every day, as a matter of course, to make your life more safe. Perhaps you lock the doors as soon as you get into your car. Maybe you have installed an alarm in your home. Or perhaps you think twice before walking around by yourself at night, and if you do go out, you are conscious of who else is on the street. In short, most of us take safety precautions all of the time; they are a part of our daily routine.

While we almost take for granted such day to day foresight as a part of our lives, for many of us, business travel presents a new set of circumstances that we don't deal with on a daily basis. Yet, as with day to day activities, business travel also requires certain precautions.

For starters, many people travel alone on business, while for leisure they more often have traveling companions. Even when you are not traveling solo, business trips may find you in unfamiliar territories, often large cities. And it's important to note that your business responsibilities can mandate activities that you might not normally undertake, such as going out alone at night, or taking a cab to an unfamiliar destination.

This book covers the following areas of business travel safety:

- **General Business Travel Tips**
- **Safe Appearances**
- **Driving Safety**
- **Air Travel Safety**
- **Train Travel Safety**
- **Taxi Safety**
- **Hotel Safety**
- **Big City Safety**
- **Safety Devices**
- **International Travel**
- **Useful Numbers**

The truth is that many hotels, airlines and other travel industries are reluctant to raise security as an issue. Those businesses that do address your safety should be commended for their honesty and concern for their customers, yet they are few and far between. That's why it's important for *you* to take a proactive stance in guarding your safety and well-being during your business travels.

Rather than state the obvious, compiled herein are some lesser-known but useful ideas specifically for safe *business* travel. Along the way you will also find *"Road Tips,"* real-life advice and anecdotes from safety experts, as well as from frequent traveler executives who spend, in some cases, 80% of their time working on the road.

We know that criminals are opportunistic: they look for easy marks. This book is about learning how to take yourself out of that category as best you can, and orienting yourself towards thinking about safety during your business trips. In doing so, you will find that you can gear these tips and ideas towards your own needs, and even come up with a few personal safety tips that work for you.

Finally, it is important to note that safety precautions can be more time-consuming and are sometimes more expensive than throwing caution to the wind. Throughout this handbook, you will see a few recommendations about additional financial costs in taking these safety steps. Fortunately, these days most companies and business travelers are aware that a small increase in cost is worth the payoff of a safe business trip.

Remember, don't be scared, be prepared.

1

General Business Travel Tips

What follows are some general ideas which, when implemented, can make your business trips smoother and safer. Most of these suggestions can and should be implemented *before* you hit the road.

Scheduling Your Business Trip

• If you feel uncomfortable traveling at night, or are going to an unfamiliar destination, plan your schedule so that you arrive during daylight hours.

• Similarly, if you feel uncomfortable meeting with business associates at night, arrange for breakfast or lunch meetings.

• Give your itinerary to your secretary or a colleague. It's always a good idea for at least one other person to know your entire schedule. That way, the person with your itinerary can locate you at all times, and will be alerted if you don't arrive where and when you are scheduled.

Packing

• Travel as lightly as possible to avoid being distracted or preoccupied with your baggage. Ship bulky papers or presentation materials ahead to the hotel or office where you will be working. It's easier and safer.

• Clothing can and should be comfortable yet still professional. Women should avoid high heels, and both sexes should wear comfortable clothing that is easy to move in.

• Pare down your wallet. Carry only the identification and credit cards you are likely to use.

Telephone Calling Card/Credit Card Safety

• Safeguard your calling card/credit card numbers in public. Credit card and calling card theft has been on the rise, especially in airports and train stations of major cities. Thieves have obtained credit card numbers by doing everything from scavenging discarded receipts to overhearing people give out their credit card numbers over the telephone. Similarly, calling card numbers have been stolen by watching over the shoulder of callers as they input their number into the phone. The following road tips suggest how you can combat this theft.

Road Tip

A pension advisor from California tells of having her calling card number stolen via binoculars as she punched it into a telephone. To guard against this, cover the keypad as you punch in your calling or credit card numbers, and check around you before you speak the numbers out loud.

Road Tip

*Tone dialers are small devices that fit over a telephone mouthpiece, and allow you to discretely punch calling card numbers into a phone's mouthpiece, rather than the more visible keypad. Two tone dialers to consider are **Magellan's** catalog device (800-962-4943), and the Budget Pocket Tone Dialer available at **Radio Shack** stores.*

• Consider keeping a log of your calling card usage, so you know when you made your last call.

Travel Insurance

• Many insurance companies offer travel insurance that can cover you for things like canceled flights (both by you and the airline), lost luggage, air or ground accidents, and medical costs abroad. However, it is important to note that you may already have the coverage you seek. For instance, many credit card companies offer insurance on items or services purchased with their cards. Also, your homeowner's policy may cover items lost or stolen while on a trip, and your existing medical coverage may include emergency medical expenses abroad. If you are interested in obtaining travel insurance, ask your insurance company for referrals to agencies that offer it, and check your existing policies and credit card company agreements to be sure additional travel insurance is not redundant.

Miscellaneous Safety Ideas

• Keeping several one dollar bills and some change in your pocket for tips and pay phones eliminates the need to dig through your purse or wallet in public. In general, it's a good idea to avoid opening your purse and/or wallet in busy public places. Standing around with an open purse or openly displaying your wallet is an invitation to would-be purse snatchers and muggers.

• Consider carrying a small flashlight in your briefcase. Frequent travelers mention incidences from hotel blackouts to subway failures as times when they were glad they had a flashlight handy.

• If you are attending a conference, remove your name tag between sessions, especially when out on the street.

Outside of convention centers and hotels it is common to see people walking around with their name tags still pinned to their lapels. While inside a meeting, name tags can be a necessity; outside they not only show that you are probably from out of town, but they give would-be thieves and con artists the advantage of knowing your name and, in some cases, where you live.

• In the same vein, do not carry conference bags or promotional materials out onto the street. Pack them away in your briefcase.

• Be alert. Stay aware of your surroundings and the goings-on of people around you. Plan what you would do in an emergency situation. Many people lose valuable seconds during an emergency when they freeze up and cannot think of what steps to take.

Road Tip

Executives who travel with portable computers might be interested in **The Sentinel***, a security cable for laptop and notebook computers. The Sentinel attaches to your computer disc drive lock and operates with a key, and can be looped around any stationary post. You can use it to avoid having your computer stolen from sites such as conference rooms, train cars, hotel rooms, or aboard planes. Available from American Data Mart at 212-755-0650.*

2

Safe
Appearances

Successful business people know that your appearance can send a strong message. Business travel presents this appearance challenge: how do you project a confident, successful image without drawing to yourself undue attention and the eyes of thieves and troublemakers? Here are some rules of thumb to go by.

• No flashy jewelry. People often wear expensive and/or flashy jewelry on a daily basis, but you should not do so on business trips. Diamond wedding rings, pearl necklaces, and shiny gold jewelry attract the attention of muggers.

Road Tip
On business trips many women forgo their wedding and engagement rings in favor of a less expensive and less flashy plain gold or silver band.

• Invest in a cheap watch. These days, it is easy to find an inexpensive wrist watch that is suitable for business attire. Advantages: you won't mind so much if you lose it, and muggers will be less likely to assault you to obtain it.

• Keep travel accoutrements to a minimum, or out of sight. Since travelers can be disoriented and unaware of their surroundings, they are often targeted for muggings and other crimes. Therefore, keep the items that scream "out-of-towner", such as maps and cameras, away from view. If you must have your camera, map, or other travel items with you, conceal them in a purse, briefcase, or pack.

• Better yet, ditch the purse or briefcase. If possible, once business is over, get rid of your purse and/or briefcase.

Road Tip

*Money belts and pouches are a harder-to-swipe alternative to purses and wallets. **Magellan's** catalog (800-962-4943) offers several models from which to choose.*

Road Tip for Women

Often women in large cities carry their money, keys and ID in their pockets. A hotel key can be left at the front desk for your return, rather than carrying it with you. If you must carry a purse, keep it zipped or snapped shut at all times, and strap it across your body diagonally. During cool weather, carry your purse under your coat or jacket.

Road Tip for Men

Do not carry your wallet in a back pocket, where it can easily be picked. Carry your wallet in your front pants pockets or breast pocket, or take the above tip and carry just your ID and whatever money you need in your pocket, leaving your wallet in a safe place.

• Women should avoid tight skirts and high heels, which limit mobility and can be perceived as symbols of weakness.

3

Driving Safety

Whether you are renting a car or using your own, driving presents a myriad of potentially dangerous circumstances with which you should be familiar. One of the most frightening possible circumstances is carjacking, i.e. a violent confrontation to steal your car. With the increased number of car alarms and other anti-theft devices, autos are getting more difficult to steal, and thieves who formerly would target unattended parked cars are now finding that carjacking is the only way to get the cars they want. But carjacking is not the only crime on the road. The following guidelines are meant to steer you clear of all kinds of driving-related crimes.

Renting a Car

There have been several well-publicized crimes against tourists who were identified as out-of-towners by their rental cars. Criminals target travelers for a variety of reasons. Travelers often carry large amounts of cash, seldom carry weapons, and are generally not aware of their surroundings. In addition, they are less likely than locals to return to the site of a crime and testify in court. Often assailants wait until the last flights of the night have arrived at the airport, then drive around from one airport car-rental agency to another, looking for an easy target.

Rental car agencies have not taken this problem lightly. In recent years, most agencies have removed the many promotional stickers and decals from their rental cars that easily marked them "rentals". However, in some states rental cars must have the word "lease" on their license plates, or prefixes that start with a particular letter. Rental agencies are lobbying state governments to change these laws, but be aware that even without bumper stickers that give the name of your rental agency, vehicles in some states still offer clues to criminals looking to target travelers.

• Be sure your rental agency has removed all stickers or other decals that identify the car as a rental, and therefore you as a traveler. Request cars without such stickers or markings.

• Make sure the rental agency is on site at the airport or station at which you are arriving. It can be an unpleasant surprise to find out, once you arrive in town, that your rental agency is a shuttle or taxi ride away from you. Plus, it's safer to avoid unnecessary modes of transportation and go directly from your train or plane to your rental car. However, if your flight is arriving late at night, you may prefer to take a taxi or airport shuttle to your hotel, then rent a car in town the next day.

• Avoid arriving at night.

• Whenever possible, drive with a colleague. Is someone arriving at the airport at approximately the same time as you? Consider teaming up and renting a car together.

• In an unfamiliar city, ask the rental agency to mark on a map the locations of police and fire stations nearest you.

• The major car rental companies have equipped anywhere from 50% - 80% of their fleets with driver-side air bags. Anti-lock brakes are also being installed in a good portion of most rental car fleets. If these features are important to you, you may request them when you order your rental car.

• Consider renting a portable cellular phone, which most rental firms in major cities offer. You will have quick access to help in case of an emergency.

Filling Up

• Try to gas up during the daylight hours.

• Having someone pump your gas for you is less dangerous (but more expensive) than getting out of your car and pumping and paying.

• If you do pump your own gas, try to frequent stations that offer pay-at-the-pump credit card service. Many of the large oil companies now offer this amenity, which allows you a quick, easy way to pay while staying near your automobile.

General Driving Safety

• Consider joining the **American Automobile Association (AAA)**, which entitles you to emergency road service anywhere in the United States. The AAA also offers insurance, travel services, and free road maps to members. For information on AAA membership, call 800-765-4222.

• Always keep your vehicle in good working condition. A reliable car is one of the most important driving safety factors. Be sure to check your vehicle's engine oil and transmission fluid regularly, and especially before a long road trip.

• Never leave personal information, such as address books,

in your vehicle.

• Do not leave any items visible in your car (jackets, purses, bags, etc.) when you park it. Items left in cars are magnets for theft.

• Keep your keys in hand while walking to your car. Do not get caught fumbling with your keys.

• If there is someone loitering near your car as you approach it, keep walking until they leave. If they do not leave the area around your vehicle, call for help.

• Before entering your car, check to be sure no one is in the back seat.

• Keep small change in the glove compartment for emergency phone calls and toll booths.

• Always keep your car keys separate from your home keys. Or obtain a valet key so that when leaving your car with an attendant, your home keys cannot be duplicated.

• Know how to get to where you are going. Study your route ahead of time, to eliminate the need to look at a map while driving.

• Keep car doors locked while driving, and keep windows up in unfamiliar areas. If it is hot and you have no air conditioning, roll the window down enough to get air, but not enough for an arm to get in the car.

Road Tip

Some ambulance personnel report that it can be difficult to rescue people from their cars when all the doors are locked. While it is still advisable to keep doors locked on city streets, you may prefer to leave only the driver side door unlocked for freeway driving.

• While driving, keep your wallet, purse or briefcase hidden, either under the seat or in the trunk. However, once you have parked your car, never leave valuables like wallets or purses inside the vehicle, even in the trunk.

• Park in well-lit areas. If you need to use a pay phone or purchase gasoline, stop where the attendants can see you.

• Do not be tricked into getting out of your car. If you are rear-ended in a remote or dark area and feel uneasy about getting out of your car to exchange insurance information, motion to the other driver to follow you to a police or fire station, or a 24-hour store.

• Do not stop for flashing white lights. Law enforcement vehicles use red flashers or blue and white ones. If you have any question about the validity of a police officer who stops you, do not get out of your car. Politely ask that the officer escort you to the nearest police station to deal with the complaint there. Don't worry about offending the officer, most will understand your fears.

• Drive in the middle lane if you feel insecure in a certain area. Try not to get in a lane where you can easily be cut off. If a car blocks you intentionally, honk repeatedly for help, but do not get out of your car.

• Be wary of people approaching your car asking for directions, change, or handing out flyers. If someone suspicious approaches your car, drive away carefully, even if it means going against a traffic rule.

• In unfamiliar areas, avoid idling your car in neutral. Keep the car in gear even when you are at a stop, in case you need to move quickly.

• Never pick up hitchhikers.

• If possible, avoid driving alone, especially at night.

Road Tip

A Colorado trucking company executive suggests that women traveling alone avoid the interstate freeways at night. If you are a woman and you must drive on an interstate at night, wear a man's cap to help disguise yourself.

Road Tip

Safe-T-Man *is a life-size rag doll for drivers fearful of being victimized while driving alone. The dummies are available in two skin tones and two age ranges. You can purchase a Safe-T-Man by calling Harbor House at (800) 9-SAFETY. Beware: highway patrols warn against using Safe-T-Man to ride in car pool lanes!*

• If you are told or signaled by a passing person that something is wrong with your car, but you feel nothing is wrong, do not stop immediately. Drive to the nearest service station or well-lighted public area to check on the condition of your vehicle.

• Your car can be a two-ton weapon. Use it, but only if absolutely necessary.

• Even if you are leaving your car for just a moment, always lock it and take the keys. This may sound like obvious advice, but consider the following data:

Road Fact

According to the International Association of Auto Theft Investigators, half of the 1.6 million cars stolen in 1992 were not locked, and one in five had keys in them.

• Consider investing in a portable phone (many businesses will contribute or pay for one) that can come in handy if your vehicle becomes disabled. Portable phones differ from permanent car phones in that they can be used in your car, as well as elsewhere. Beware that the antenna for a permanent car phone may make your vehicle a target for theft, while portable phones cannot be as easily detected.

Road Tip

Security consultants suggest that a good way to determine if you are being followed is to make three consecutive right turns. If the car tailing yours stays behind you, you are right to assume you are being followed.

If You Think You Are Being Followed

• Stay in your car. If you have a cellular phone with you, call the police and tell them that you are being followed.

• Avoid turning down unfamiliar streets, which could lead to dead ends.

• Do not drive home. Try to find a police or fire station. If that fails, drive to a busy location where there are a lot of other people. Stay in your car and honk your horn until help arrives.

If Your Car Breaks Down

• Attach a handkerchief or some type of cloth to the antenna. Turn on your emergency flashers. Raise your hood. Then, *stay inside the car with the windows up and doors locked.*

• Keep your seat belt fastened while waiting for help. Disabled vehicles have been hit by oncoming cars, even when parked on the shoulder with lights flashing and hoods raised.

• If someone stops to help, do not open the doors or windows to communicate with them. Ask them to call or send for help.

• Do not accept a ride to get help.

• If you see someone else in need of assistance, do not stop. As you drive by, signal the motorist that you will get help, then go to a telephone and call the police.

• If you are confronted, many experts advise giving the attackers what they want. Often violence occurs when citizens resist a carjacking or mugging, and certainly no possession is more valuable than your life.

Useful Number

• For more information about traffic safety, call the **National Highway Administration's Office of Travel Safety** at 202-366-2540.

Driving Safety Check List

The following safety items are recommended for you to carry by the United States Department of Transportation and the National Safety Council.

In the glove compartment:

• Automobile registration

• Insurance documents

• Telephone number of someone to call in an emergency

• Health insurance card

• Flashlight

In the trunk:

• Spare tire, properly inflated

• Jack and lug wrench for changing tires

- Fire extinguisher
- First aid kit
- Flares or reflective devices
- <u>Empty</u> gas can, approved by the fire department
- Battery jumper cables

4

Air Travel
Safety

In general, air travel is a safe, efficient way to travel long distances. In fact, your time in the air can be the safest part of your business trip. Often, it is the other places associated with airports—parking lots, baggage areas, and terminals—where you need to be especially on guard. While airport security officers take stringent measures to protect travelers, heeding the following advice can decrease your chances of being a victim.

• Try to avoid checking your luggage. You will sidestep lost or stolen baggage, and avoid standing around alone at the baggage pick-up area. Plus, less baggage makes you more mobile and you will get to your destination more quickly.

• The Air Transport Association estimates that three out of every 100,000 checked bags are pilfered by baggage handlers. This may be a conservative estimate, since many bags mistakenly thought of as lost are actually stolen. Additionally, you should know that $1,250 is the most an airline will pay you for a lost or stolen bag inside the United States (if your bag is lost or stolen outside of the U.S. the amount per bag is $460), and there may be exemptions for jewelry and electronic equipment.

If you must check baggage, take the following advice:

• Never check valuables, be their importance sentimental or monetary.

• Keep pharmaceutical prescriptions, important work, and travel documents in your purse, briefcase, or carry-on luggage.

• Always use luggage locks. While baggage handlers who want to break into your bags assert that locks do not always stop them, they are a deterrent. **Lewis N. Clark** (800-621-8083) offers a variety of such locks as well as useful traveler's cable lock.

• Do not travel with flashy, expensive, name-brand luggage. This attracts attention and leads thieves to believe there may be something worth stealing inside.

• Consider wrapping your checked bags with tape or rope. Also Lewis N. Clark (800-621-8083) sells a locking "Trav-A-Belt" for luggage security.

Road Tip

The Miami airport now offers a service of shrink-wrapping your checked baggage, for a small fee. Watch for other airports that will soon be testing this service.

• Keep an eye on your carry-on luggage. Never leave it unattended. While seated or standing, put your arm or leg through a strap.

• Never agree to carry anything for someone else on board or in your luggage. You may unsuspectingly be carrying a bomb, or smuggling drugs or other illegal items.

Road Tip

El Al Airlines, the carrier from Israel, is known worldwide for its excellent security. Typically, a trained security agent questions each passenger before boarding an El Al flight, to be sure, among other things, that the passenger has not unwittingly been asked to take part in a terrorist act. For instance, security agents will query,

"Has anyone asked you to deliver a gift to a loved one when you arrive at your destination?". "Did anyone deliver a package to you at your hotel before you left, such as an item purchased at a store earlier in the day?"

• If you see an unattended briefcase, suitcase or package, notify security immediately.

• Keep a close watch on your tickets as you wait to board the plane. Do not leave them out in the open where it may be easy for a stranger to read them, and if you are holding your tickets in your hand or breast pocket, make sure your name is not showing.

• Use airport shuttles to access parking lots, rather than walking alone.

Road Tip

Travelers loaded down with baggage are inviting targets for attack in airport parking lots. A Los Angeles publisher always has the parking lot shuttle drop him off right next to his car, rather than walking to his vehicle alone.

• If you travel frequently, consider joining airline clubs, which offer private, secure waiting areas and restrooms, as well as complimentary business services and refreshments. Remember that a well-rested traveler is a safer, more alert one as well. Following is a listing of the major airlines' private clubs:

• **American Admirals Clubs** offer annual membership for $250, and lifetime memberships for $2,600. For more information, call 800-237-7971.

• **Continental Presidents Clubs** offer annual memberships for $200 single or $275 with a spouse, three-year memberships for $425 single or $575 with a spouse, or a lifetime membership for $1,825. For more information, call 800-322-2640.

• **Delta Crown Rooms** offer annual memberships for $150 single or $200 with a spouse, and three-year memberships for $360 or $460 with a spouse. For more information, call 800-323-2323.

• **Northwest World Clubs** offer annual memberships for $225, renewals for $175. For more information, call 612-727-5798.

• **TWA Ambassador Clubs** offer annual memberships for $150 single or $175 with spouse, three-year memberships for $300 single or $375 with spouse, or lifetime memberships for $1,500 single or $1,750 with spouse. For more information, call 800-325-4815.

• **United Red Carpet Clubs** offer annual memberships for $210. For more information, call 800-647-5656.

• **US Air Clubs** offer annual memberships for $200 single or $250 with a spouse, three-year memberships for $425 single or $575 with a spouse, or lifetime memberships for $2,000 single or $3,000 with a spouse. For more information, call 800-428-4322.

Road Tip

Sometimes fellow travelers seize the opportunity of sitting next to you on a long flight as a chance to make unwanted advances. If the person next to you is making you feel uncomfortable or unsafe, report his/her behavior to the flight crew immediately, then switch seats.

When Tagging Your Luggage

• Consider using your business address and telephone number on tags, rather than your home contact information. An exception is in foreign countries potentially hostile to the United States (such as parts of the Middle East), where no identification indicating that a passenger is American or employed by an American company should be visible. This precaution should be taken to avoid a possible kidnapping.

• Use just your first initial, not your entire first name. While it is important to have identification on your luggage in case it is lost or stolen, it is equally important to avoid giving personal information to strangers.

• Keep your luggage tags covered in public places, or invest in "privacy tags", which have a removable flap that covers your name and address.

• In addition to tagging the outside of your luggage, paste a label with your last name and address inside your bags, in case the tags fall off.

Air Travel Health

• Exercise on long flights. Get up and walk around the aisles, or stand in the rear or near the exit doors and stretch. Moving around will stimulate your blood flow and bring oxygen to your brain.

Road Tip
If you tend to get motion sickness, try to be seated at the center of the plane near the wings, where movement of the plane is felt the least.

• Try to be awake when the plane descends to land. As the plane descends, the air pressure in the cabin increases. If you are awake your body reacts to the change by swallowing and thus equalizing the air pressure in your head and in the cabin. If you are asleep, you swallow less frequently and risk damaging your eardrums or other discomfort as the plane descends.

Road Tip

Drink at least 8 ounces of water for each hour of the flight. Long flights pull moisture out of your body, as does the consumption of alcohol on board. Rehydrating your body during a flight will make you feel better during and after the flight. Also, avoid salty food such as salted peanuts.

Useful Numbers

• For airline complaints or information, call the **United States Department of Transportation** at 202-366-2220.

• To register a complaint about a safety hazard, call the **Federal Aviation Administration** at 202-267-3481.

• For instructions regarding the air shipment of hazardous material, The Federal Aviation Administration asks that you contact your airline representative.

• For an annual fee of $99, the **International Airline Passenger Association (IAPA)** gives members advice regarding compensation for flight delays and cancellations, ticket refunds, and lost, damaged, or stolen luggage plus discounted travel opportunities. They can be reached at 800-821-4272.

5

Train Travel Safety

Especially for short jaunts, trains can be a convenient and inexpensive alternative to air travel. Many business people prefer the rails to planes, since trains offer flexible schedules and mobility while on board. In addition, executives say that they can get more work done while riding trains, as opposed to the more cramped quarters on airplanes.

However, train stations and trains themselves can be the location of scams and crimes. Anyone can walk into a train depot, and the hustle-bustle of train stations make them an ideal spot for pick-pocketing and purse snatching. Security in train stations is usually less stringent than in airports, and the use of security devices like metal detectors is rare. Your best bet is to be on guard and follow these few tips.

• Never leave your baggage unattended in the station.

• Keep your purse or briefcase in sight, either next to you or on your lap. Purses or briefcases placed under your seat can easily be nudged away from behind you.

Road Tip

Beware of scams by other passengers. Sometimes people work in teams to steal your belongings on trains. One person pretends to have dropped his keys or contact lens. While you and the other passengers are being Good

Samaritans and "helping" the passenger look for the lost item, the partner swipes your purse, wallet, and other valuables. If a fellow passenger asks for your help in locating their lost item, tell him to ask a porter for assistance.

• Sleeping compartments can only be locked from inside. While you are in your sleeping car, keep the door locked. If you leave your sleeper to go to the dining car, restroom, or lounge take all valuables with you, as the compartment cannot be locked from the outside.

Road Tip

Beware of scam artists on train platforms or in the train cars who claim they were just mugged or lost their wallet and need "only enough money for a ticket." While the story may sound sad, it is most likely untrue.

6

Taxi
Safety

Getting into a taxi cab can sometimes feel like a crap-shoot. As if arriving in an unfamiliar city isn't unnerving enough, often you find that you need to take a taxi to your final destination. In effect, that means getting into a car alone with a stranger, something your primary instincts tell you is potentially dangerous.

In fact, most business travelers report little or no trouble dealing with taxis on their travels. One executive left her carry-on bag in the back seat of a taxi in Manhattan, only to have the driver return it, intact, to her hotel 20 minutes later, once he noticed she had left it behind.

The key to safe and relaxed taxi travel is to follow this simple advice.

• Only use the sanctioned taxi stands outside airports and train stations. Do not get into a car with someone purporting to be a taxi driver. Often people hang around airports to offer rides, even though they are not licensed taxi cabs. (Licensed taxi drivers must undergo personal background checks and driving safety courses prior to obtaining their licenses.)

Road Tip
In many cities, licensed taxis have identifying marks on the outside of the cars. For example, in New York City licensed cabs have special medallions on the hood, and in Washington, D.C., a visor band denotes a license.

Ask the taxi stand managers at airports and train stations what demarks the licensed cabs in the city you are working in, then ride in only those cabs.

• Try to cab share. If you meet someone on your trip or in a cab line with whom you feel safe and who is heading to the same part of town as you, consider asking if they would like to share a cab. It is cheaper, and safer, to travel in a group.

• Check out the cab before your enter it. Do the door handles work? Do the windows wind down properly?

• Try to determine ahead of time the amount of time and money the ride will take.

Road Tip

A Chicago attorney asks the hotel concierge or airline personnel how much time and what approximate fare a taxi ride to her destination will be. If the ride varies in time or fare by a great extent, she knows the driver is taking advantage of her, and she asks to get out of the cab at a safe spot.

• If you find a taxi driver whom you like, ask for his/her card, and use him/her on future visits, as illustrated in the following road tip. Especially in smaller cities, cab drivers are often happy to make pre-arrangements with you for future fares.

Road Tip

A San Francisco-based consultant who travels to several cities on a regular basis tells that when she finds female cab drivers, she takes their cards. The next time she knows she is coming to that city, she calls ahead and the driver meets her flight.

• Try to carry your baggage in the back seat with you,

rather than in the trunk. That way, if you feel unsafe and need to exit the cab quickly, you can grab your bags and leave, rather than having them held hostage in the trunk.

Road Tip

According to an article in "U.S. News and World Report," one way to lessen the possibility of being cheated by a cab driver in a strange city is to act like you've been there before. When providing the driver with your destination, say "The Clift" or "The Biltmore". Using the proper names "Four Seasons Clift Hotel" or "The Arizona Biltmore" is a sure sign that you are an out-of-towner.

• Wear your safety belt. While most people wear their seat belt when driving in their own automobiles, many fail to wear seat belts in taxis. In fact, in many states, mandatory seat belt laws exempt rear-seat passengers in cabs. Nonetheless, a combination of taxi driver recklessness and not wearing a seat belt leave passengers at a high risk for blunt trauma to the head and neck.

Road Fact

A two-year study of injured cab passengers admitted to the emergency department at Lennox Hill Hospital in New York City documented fractures of the larynx, nasal bone, external ear canal and neck, and lacerated and paralyzed vocal cords. All the patients were injured in collisions with other vehicles. None of the patients was wearing a seat belt.

• If your driver is driving too fast or recklessly, don't be afraid or embarrassed to ask him/her to slow down or be careful. After all, *you* are paying for the ride.

• Keep an eye on the meter. If the device makes unusually

large jumps, ask the driver what's going on. Unscrupulous cabbies have been known to tamper with meters.

• Keep cash in your pocket, to avoid having to open your wallet and/or purse in the back of the cab.

• If a taxi is dropping you off at a location that makes you feel insecure, ask the driver to wait and watch while you gain access to the building.

Road Tip

If you are unhappy with your cab driver's service, but are afraid to confront him/her in person, ask for a receipt for the ride. In most cities, cab receipts record the meter number of the cab in which you rode, so that you can contact the cab company and tell them which driver you have a complaint about.

• In some cities, limousines are almost as affordable as taxis. Call ahead and check, and if possible utilize a limousine service. Likewise, check with your hotel to see if they offer shuttle or limousine service.

• If you are afraid to ride in a cab alone, look into the airport shuttle services. Most carry groups of people by van to different parts of the city, and often the service is less expensive (though more time-consuming) than taking a taxi.

7

Hotel
Safety

Much has been reported on how even the finest hotels fail to take basic security measures. The combination of easy access to guest rooms and off-guard travelers make hotel guests marks for theft, rape, and assault. Too often, hotel guests have a relaxed attitude about safety, and are lulled into a false sense of security by their elegant surroundings and promises of round-the-clock luxury service. Don't check your common sense at the door; you must assume responsibility for protecting yourself while staying in hotels.

Choosing A Hotel

• Ask your colleagues for recommendations on good hotels in safe neighborhoods.

• Call ahead and query the management about the safety features of the hotel, such as magnetic card strip locks (which are recoded for each guest), in-room safes, closed-circuit television monitoring of halls, safe-deposit boxes, and well-lit corridors and parking lots.

• Choose a hotel that has a business center (faxes, copiers, computers, telexes, etc.) in house, so you don't need to leave the hotel for your business needs. Better yet, some hotels now offer business amenities in the room, like lap-top computer hookups, phones with multiple lines, voice mail, newspaper delivery, and fax machines or quick fax delivery. If you intend to conduct a lot of business from your room, ask your hotel if they offer a business traveler's package. Many chains now offer such plans, which typically cost $10 to $20 more than the regular room rate, but offer business amenities like unlimited local telephone calls and faxes, late-evening snacks, and health-club privileges. Some business travelers find that they save money on their hotel bills by taking advantage of these packages, rather than paying for each of the services on an a la carte basis.

• Determine if the hotel offers club or concierge floors, which often have staff on the floor round-the-clock.

• Make sure the hotel offers room service hours that suit your needs, so you are not forced to go out to get food if you prefer the safety of your room.

• Inquire if the hotel has complimentary limousine service. This may sound like an unnecessary luxury, but it is a safety measure as well to have assured transport to and from airports and/or meetings.

Choosing A Bed & Breakfast

• Some business people opt for bed & breakfast accommodations, which they feel offer more personal (and therefore safer) service. Travelers report that they become familiar with the bed & breakfast staff, and are assured that their personal safety requests will be carried out.

• Query the management about the inn's safety features. Is there a secure, well-lit parking area? Is a staff member on site at all times? Are there dead bolts on the guest room doors?

• Ask your colleagues in the area if the inn is located in a safe neighborhood.

• Ask if the inn is listed in the American Automobile Association (AAA) directory, since the AAA has stringent requirements, in order for bed & breakfasts and country inns to be listed in their directory. The requirements include:

• A locking mechanism that allows a guest to lock the door when leaving the room

• A dead bolt inside the room

• Dead bolts on doors that connect to other doors

• Locking devices on sliding doors, and doors to walkways and common balconies

Checking In

• If someone is nearby as you check in, do not allow your name and/or room number to be stated out loud. One way to insure that your personal information is not stated is illustrated in the following road tip.

> ### Road Tip
> *One hotelier tells of a woman who has a preprinted card that says "Hello, my name is Jane Doe. I have a reservation and am here to check in. Please do not state my name or room number out loud."*

• When filling out the guest registration card, use your first initial, rather than your full first name.

• Try to avoid ground floor rooms and rooms with doors that open to the outside, which are easier for intruders to break in to.

• Request a room near the elevator, to avoid walking alone

down long corridors. If no such room is available, ask the hotel to provide an escort to your room.

• Always use a bellhop to escort you to your room. He/she will enter your room, and check the closets and bathroom to be sure no one is there. Check the door locks while the bellhop is still in the room, and in general, do not let him/her go until you feel your room is secure. While it will cost you a small tip, it is worth it to ensure that your room is unoccupied.

Road Tip

A Minneapolis consultant for an accounting firm once checked into a room to find that all the chain locks in the hotel were installed upside down, and automatically unlocked. Be sure your room is secure, by testing all locking mechanisms when you first arrive.

• If no bellhop is available to check your room before you enter, take the following road tip from airline staff:

Road Tip

Airline personnel are trained to put their luggage in the doorjamb, to leave the door ajar, and check behind the shower curtain, in the closet, and under the bed before they stay in a hotel room.

While You Are A Guest

• If your room door features a peephole and a dead bolt, use them.

• If you have not called for service and someone arrives at your door, call the front desk to confirm that they have been sent by hotel management. Even if someone purporting to be on the hotel staff calls and says they are coming to fix or check on something in your room (i.e. your air conditioner, smoke alarm, telephone, television), call the front desk to make sure that they have actually been sent by the hotel management. If the front desk does not confirm your report, immediately have the clerk send hotel security to your room.

Road Tip

Hotel house phones are often used by criminals who pretend to be on the hotel staff to gain access to your room. Sometimes potential assailants will try to determine if you are alone in your room by asking you if the room is being used for a "double or single occupancy". Beware, rapists and thieves have easily entered hotel rooms under the auspices of being on the hotel staff.

• If you need maintenance or assistance in your room, ask for the name of the person being sent up to your room, and request their name when they arrive, before you open the door. If it is not the same name, do not open the door. Call downstairs to the front desk and ask for assistance.

• If you have called for room service, ask the deliverer to slide your receipt under the door before you open it, to prove the person is actually from room service.

• If you need maid service, ask for it at the front desk on your way out, rather than leaving a hang tag on your door. A hang tag requesting maid service is like an advertisement that your room is presently unoccupied.

Road Tip

A Los Angeles-based flight attendant says that if her room has already been cleaned and she is going out, she leaves the "Do Not Disturb" sign on her door handle and the TV and lights on, so people think the room is still occupied.

• If an associate is meeting you at your hotel, arrange to meet him/her in the lobby, not in your room. Your associate can call up to your room from the lobby phone once he or she arrives, or you can wait for your appointments downstairs in the lobby. The point is, do not invite someone to be alone with you in your hotel room, even a colleague.

• Do not assume that because someone is dressed in a uniform, they are on the hotel staff. Creative criminals can obtain uniforms that appear to be that of hotel staff, then roam hotels freely committing crimes.

Road Tip

An accountant walked out of a conference at an Atlanta hotel, handed his car keys to a uniformed valet, and told him to bring up his black BMW from the garage. Trouble was, the uniformed man wasn't really a hotel valet, and he promptly stole the car.

• Turn in your keys at the front desk before going out to conduct business. This reduces the risk that you will lose your keys or that someone will steal them from you.

• Avoid leaving credit card receipts or your hotel reservation receipt laying around in the room.

• When returning to your hotel late at night, use the main entrance.

• Make sure that any sliding glass doors, windows, or connecting room doors are locked. Likewise, be sure your room door is firmly closed.

• Always use the chain lock on your hotel door, not just while you are sleeping, but anytime you are in your room.

Road Tip

After checking into a Philadelphia hotel, an executive entered his room, and walked in on two sleeping people. The hotel had mistakenly double booked the room. The unfortunate fact is that hotels are not uniformly careful in giving out room keys, and a simple chain lock can protect you from intruders.

• If the locks alone don't seem sufficient, pull a chair up to the door while you sleep. Or, consider carrying a simple doorstop with you, which, when wedged beneath the door, can be a very effective barrier. In addition, portable travel locks can be purchased at most department stores and can provide an additional lock for your hotel door.

Road Tip

Magellan's catalog offers three types of gadgets designed to make your hotel rooms more secure. One is an alarm that attaches to your hotel room door. Another is a combination lock that you can use to lock yourself into your room. This device comes with an adjustable plate hook that can keep intruders out even if the lock is not snapped shut, in case you need to exit quickly in the event of a fire or other emergency. The third alarm is modeled like a doorstop, and once in place, it sounds if your door is opened. Call 800-962-4943 to receive a copy of the catalog.

Safety For Your Valuables

• Keep your bags locked when you are not using them, and leave them in the closet.

• Do not bring valuables on your business trips. Simply stated, this is the best way to ensure the safety of your valuable belongings.

• If you must bring valuables, do not leave them in your

room, unless it features a room safe. Consider using your hotel's safe or security boxes. In most cases, hotels are not legally responsible for cash, jewelry, and other valuables that are stolen out of your room.

• If you require use of your hotel's safe or security boxes, do not ask for this service at the front desk. Discussing your need for a safe box in the lobby calls attention to yourself, and raises a red flag to thieves and muggers that you have valuables in your room or on your person. Instead, call down from the privacy of your room to procure use of the hotel's safe.

Fire Safety In Hotels

In 1990, the federal government enacted the Hotel and Motel Fire Safety Act. The Act establishes the following fire prevention and control guidelines:

• Installation of a smoke detector meeting the National Fire Protection Association (NFPA) Standard in each guest room; and

• Installation of an automatic sprinkler in accordance with the NFPA Standard in each place of public accommodation. The sprinkler system is required to be installed in each guest room and all common areas of each facility. Facilities that are three stories or lower are exempt from this sprinkler system guideline.

While the federal government does not mandate that all hotels and motels follow these guidelines, federal agencies must now ensure that no less than 65 percent of their travel accommodations for federal employee business trips be in approved facilities. The percentage increases to 75 percent five years after enactment of the Act, and to 90 percent six years after enactment of the Act. In addition, no federally funded conferences, meetings, or seminars may be held in a facility that does not meet the required safety guidelines, unless a waiver is granted by the head of the agency sponsoring or funding the event. Many private sector corporations are following suit and now require their business travelers to lodge only in hotels and motels that comply with the Act.

The Federal Emergency Management Agency (FEMA) compiles and publishes in the Federal Register a national master list of all places of public accommodation in each state that meet the safety requirements of the bill.

• Ask the reservationist if the hotel complies with the Hotel and Motel Fire Safety Act of 1990. Many luxury high-rise hotels do not comply, because the cost of fitting each room with sprinklers is prohibitive.

• As you check in, inquire about the location of the hotel's emergency exits.

• Once in your room, make sure your smoke alarm is in working order. Many smoke detectors feature a small red light which shines to indicate that the alarm is functional.

• Check to see if a fire evacuation plan is posted in your room.

Road Tip

Pick an easily accessible place in your room to leave your room key (for instance, on top of the television set or on the night table), and follow the same pattern in every hotel you frequent. That way, you can always locate your key in the middle of the night, even in a power-outage or fire.

• Report any fire or smoke to the hotel operator.

In the unlikely event of fire, take the following steps:

• If a fire starts in your room, leave immediately, close the door behind you, and notify the front desk.

• If you wake up to smoke in your room, roll to the floor and crawl out of the room.

• Move quickly and calmly to the stairs. Do not take the elevators!

• If fire breaks out and you are in your room, do not open the door until you have felt it for heat. If the door is hot, do not open it! If the door feels cool, open it slowly, but be prepared to slam it shut if fire or heavy smoke is in the hall.

• If you are forced to remain in your room, use wet towels, sheets or clothes to seal the cracks around the door. Fill the bathtub with water and use ice buckets or waste baskets to throw water on hot surfaces. Turn off the air conditioner and fan.

Useful Numbers

• **American Hotel and Motel Association**, 202-289-3100

• **Federal Emergency Mgmt. Agency**, 202-646-2500

• **National Fire Protection Association**, 703-516-4346

8

Big
City
Safety

Small towns and suburbs differ from big cities in many ways. One of the most obvious is both the perception and reality of safety. While virtually no area is 100% free from crime, residents of small towns and suburbs feel they have less need for safety precautions on a day-to-day basis than do big city dwellers.

One way to help combat trouble while you are doing business in an unfamiliar metropolis is to adopt a big city attitude. That means be alert, think quickly, and take the advice of people who are used to the potential perils of city living.

Street Smarts

You may find it easy and convenient to stay within walking distance of the office or conference center where you will conduct business. That means walking, perhaps alone, on unfamiliar streets. When walking to appointments:

• Ask your colleagues if it is safe for you to walk to meet them. If so, ask for the most direct route to your meeting.

• Call your appointments to let them know you are on your way. If you do not show up, someone will know you are missing.

• Try to walk in groups, or if you are alone, walk close behind groups you see on the street. Don't be too embarrassed to ask a safe-looking group if you can walk with them, even if you don't know them.

• Walk confidently, alertly, and purposefully. Keep your hands free. Try to look like you know where you are going, even if you don't.

Road Tip

A San Francisco marketing professional relates that in three years of living in the city, the only time she was harassed on the street was when she neglected to pay attention to her surroundings. While walking from a meeting to her car, she was reading a proposal, rather than watching who was nearby. A man approached, shoved her in the shoulder, and proceeded to chase her to her car. While she escaped injury, she firmly believes that the incident could had been avoided had she been more alert.

• Walk facing oncoming traffic, so you can see approaching cars.

• Do not respond to people who call out at you from doorways, cars, etc. You do not owe a response to anyone who asks for one.

• Walk close to the curb on well-traveled streets (unless a car pulls up), and avoid doorways, alleys, and bushes.

• Wearing earphones while walking limits your ability to sense danger signs.

• If you think you are being followed by someone on foot, cross the street and walk quickly in the other direction to a well-lit area.

• If you are being followed by someone who is driving, turn around and walk quickly in the opposite direction. If you can, get the license plate number and a description of the car.

On Public Transportation

• Ask your colleagues the safest, most direct route to your meeting.

• While waiting for a subway or bus, stand in well-lit, well-traveled areas.

• Sit near the conductor or driver.

• Strap your purse or briefcase across your body.

• Do not wear flashy jewelry. It is plain dumb to wear expensive (or even expensive-looking) jewelry on public transportation. Despite this warning, many people forget to leave fine jewelry at home, so here is a tip from someone who wears her engagement ring at all times, even while traveling.

> ### Road Tip
> *If you feel you must wear a ring with prominent stones (such as an engagement ring) or have forgotten to take it off, turn the ring so the gems face the inside of your hand, leaving only a plain band for others to see.*

• Do not make eye contact with other passengers.

• In subways, try to ride in the compartments with conductors in them.

• Most companies will pay for you to ride taxis, rather than take busses or subways. Check with your employer regarding its policy.

Dealing With Homeless People

• Never open your purse or wallet for someone on the street.

• Experts advise not to give money to people on the street, since your money may go towards drugs or alcohol. If you want to financially assist homeless people, donate to shelters, food banks, and other organizations that support them.

In Elevators

• Check the elevator before entering. If you are uncomfortable with any of the occupants, wait for the next elevator car.

• If you are waiting with a stranger for an elevator to arrive, stand away from the doorway, to avoid being pushed inside.

• Once inside the elevator, stand near the control panel, and take notice of the location of the emergency buttons. If accosted, push all the buttons, except the stop button.

• If someone in the elevator makes you feel insecure, get off at the next floor and take another car.

Using Automated Teller Machines (ATMs)

Automated teller machines are a quick and easy way to get cash in a strange city, but they can also be dangerous. Often hotels will cash checks for guests, so inquire in your hotel before you run out to a bank. If you need to use an ATM, take into account the following advice.

• Avoid using ATMs at night.

Road Fact
Contrary to what you might think, the Los Angeles

Police Department says that approximately 50% of ATM attacks are committed between the hours of 7:00 p.m. and midnight, while only 10% are committed between midnight and 4:00 a.m.

• Try to get someone to accompany you to the ATM.

• Use busy ATMs. It's worth the wait to have the safety of others around you.

• Drive-up ATMs are safer that walk-ups. When using a drive-up ATM, always keep your car running.

• Have your card ready and forms filled out before you approach the ATM.

• Safeguard your code number, as you would with a credit or calling card. Use one hand to shield the keypad as you input your card number. Always take your receipts with you; do not leave them at the ATM counter or even in the trash next to the ATM machine.

Road Tip

Two men were arrested for this complicated ATM theft. They set up a video camera (camouflaged in the back of their truck), and videotaped people entering their code numbers into the ATM machine. When ATM users left their receipts at the machine counters, the men picked them up, and then went back to the video to determine by the time recorded on the tape which PIN codes went with the account numbers recorded on the receipts. The men had counterfeit ATM cards made and coded with the ATM user's account numbers, and then had easy access to their bank accounts.

• Avoid displaying your cash. Count it after you have returned to your car or hotel.

• If you are in the middle of a transaction and you notice someone suspicious, cancel the transaction, pocket your ATM card, and leave immediately.

• If you are followed after you make a transaction, immediately go to the nearest public area.

9

Safety
Devices

There is a flood of safety devices now on the market, and what you choose is a personal decision. Keep in mind, however, that many personal security experts do not recommend the use of mace, dyes, pepper spray or similar devices, since they often result in negative, unintended consequences. For example, mace or pepper sprays can be wrestled away and used against the person carrying it, and dyes can serve to aggravate and anger assailants. In addition, you should know that federal law prohibits the air transport of mace, tear gas, and other irritants in either checked or carry-on luggage. Here are some safety devices you may want to consider:

Sound And Other Devices

Sound is an effective and safe crime deterrent. Unlike other products such as mace or weapons, sound cannot be used against you. While every situation is unique, the best way to use sound as a crime deterrent is proactively. That means if you think you might be in danger, even if you are not sure, use sound. It is better to suffer the consequences of embarrassment than be the victim of a crime.

• Your voice is an effective safety device, and it is always handy. You can use it to assert yourself, to make your wishes known, or to yell. Unfortunately, fear and shock can make it impossible to produce a sustained scream, or an attacker may be able to force you to stop screaming.

Shriek alarms and personal sirens are small, portable devices that produce high quality sound. Safety experts are increasingly recommending the use of such devices since they:

• Dramatically increase your ability to make a loud, sustained noise

• Are instant and reliable

• Create distinctive sounds that stand out.

• Alarms and sirens must be used correctly in order to increase their effectiveness.

• Check frequently to see that they are in working order.

• Carry them with you at all times. If you feel you are in a potentially dangerous situation, carry the alarm in your hand, where it can be activated instantly.

• Rely on your intuition. If you feel unsafe, you probably are, but you must rely on intuition to tell you when to activate an alarm. For example, if someone holds you up at gun point, an alarm might cause him/her to panic and shoot, rather than to run away. Use your judgment.

• Be comfortable using alarms at the first sign of danger. Unlike weapons or tear gas, you do not need to be close to your assailant for an alarm to be effective. In fact, the benefit of alarms is that you can stave off crime by using the alarm before you are assaulted.

• Many devices can be attached to your hotel door in addition to being carried with you, and will sound if the door is opened. Check to see if the device you choose has this option.

Sound safety devices are manufactured by many companies. Here are a few to check out:

• Companion, available from **The Company of Women**, 800-937-1193

• **Egis Personal Safety Systems**, 800-882-5778

• First Aid alarm/flashlight, available from **The Company of Women**, 800-937-1193

• Quorum, **Jodi Capps**, Independent Distributor, 818-224-3297

• Pocket Siren, available from **The Company of Women**, 800-937-1193

• SoundMate, available from **Safety Zone**, 800-999-3030

• Telko, available from **Safety Zone**, 800-999-3030

• Flash guns are devices that emit a blinding flash of light that temporarily disorients an attacker. While the device can be effective when an assailant is at close range, it is not useful at the first hint of trouble. For instance, if you see someone suspicious across the street who appears to be coming toward you to mug you, an alarm may help to scare off the assailant, whereas a flash of light can only disable the assailant once he/she is near you.

• **Portable telephones** give users the security of knowing they can call for help, anywhere, at any time. Portable phones are especially useful in the car, so that if you are stranded, you can call for help without leaving your vehicle. However, do not use a portable telephone on the street, where someone might mug you to steal your phone.

Counter Spy Shops are located in several cities in the United States and Europe. They specialize in security products and services, and can be found in the following cities:

- Beverly Hills, 310-274-6256

- Houston, 713-626-0007

- London, 071-408-0287

- Miami, 305-358-4336

- New York, 212-688-8500

- Washington, D.C., 202-682-5380

If You Are Attacked

If your best defensive efforts fail and you are attacked, there are many ways to respond to the situation. Since every situation is different, there is no one right way to deal with a confrontation. Factors to be considered include presence of a weapon, location of the assault, and the ratio of assailants to victims. Take the time now to consider how you would respond to an assault. Would you:

- Offer no resistance to avoid physical violence?

- Stall for time?

- Negotiate?

- Distract the assailant, then flee?

- Be verbally assertive?

- Scream to attract attention?

- Physically resist?

Experts say that it helps to continually assess the situation as it is happening. If your first strategy doesn't work, try another one. Also, try to observe as much as you can about the assailant (their clothing, hair, face, height, build, behavior, special identifying marks like scars or tattoos), to assist in filing a police report.

Useful Numbers

If you are the victim of an attack, consult local hospitals or law enforcement agencies for nearby organizations that offer counseling and support. The **National Victims Center** can provide counseling referrals for victims at their toll-free INFOLINK telephone number, **800-FYI-CALL**.

In addition, the **Coalition of Victims' Attorneys and Consultants (COVAC)** is a national referral and information service for victims seeking assistance with civil suits against perpetrators and third parties. Their telephone number for more information is (703) 276-2880.

10

International Travel

Traveling abroad for business can be challenging, exciting, and rewarding. It also presents an entirely new set of circumstances for business travelers to tackle, including language barriers, unfamiliar customs and food, possible hostility towards Americans and/or American business, and other potential travel hazards. While safety issues vary from country to country, following are some useful tips to maximize the rewards and minimize the pitfalls of international business travel.

Review your company's international travel policies. If none are in place, ask the following questions:

• Is your company a well-known American firm? If so, some companies suggest registering in hotels under assumed corporate names, to avoid hostile behavior toward American business people in countries known to be anti-American.

• Does your company have kidnap insurance? Although highly unusual, American business executives have been kidnapped for political and economic reasons.

• Learn about the customs and mores of the country you are visiting. This is a tricky area, and there have been many stories reported about business dealings gone awry due to poor communication and misread gestures. Guide books and consulates/embassies are good resources for learning about the countries in which you will be working. The following road tips offer just two examples of the importance of brushing up on international customs.

Road Tips

A woman who travels worldwide for her job with the U.S. State Department says that in many parts of South America it is perfectly acceptable for women to wear very short mini-skirts, but shorts of any length are considered scandalous.

In Japan, it is considered rude to take someone's business card and place it in your back pants pocket.

Similarly, gestures can get you into sticky situations. A gesture common and friendly to you may be considered rude or shocking by your foreign counterpart, as in the following situations:

Road Tips

The thumbs-up sign meaning "good" or "okay" to Americans and Britons is offensive in some countries such as part of the Middle East, where it means, roughly, "sit on this".

In India and parts of the Far East it is considered rude to touch one's head, while Westerners commonly pat a child's head as a sign of affection.

As the feet are the lowest part of the body, in Thailand it is extremely rude to point your feet at anybody, particularly if the gesture is deliberate. Most Thais strive to avoid doing so, and as a result you seldom see Thais with their legs crossed, or if they are, they tend to purposely point their toes to the ground.

• Consider learning a few emergency phrases in the language of the country you are visiting. Here are some phrases to memorize, or to keep with you on a pocket-sized card:

"Help!"

"Police"

"Fire"

"Where is the US Embassy?"

"I need a doctor!"

"Where is a hospital?"

"Where is a telephone?"

• **AT&T's Language Line** provides 24-hour-a-day, seven-day-a-week interpretation and translation services for more than 140 languages and dialects. A toll-free number connects callers to an interpreter who can translate an international telephone call or a conversation between participants standing in the same room. In the United States and Canada, Language Line can be reached at **800-628-8486**. The cost varies per what country you need the interpreter to call, and can be billed to a major credit card. Outside of the U.S. and Canada, you must use your long-distance calling card to place a call into the United States, then access Language Line via their 800 number.

• Most major long distance telephone companies can provide their calling card holders with a list of country-specific access codes to English-speaking operators. Sprint users can obtain Sprint Express code numbers by calling 800-877-4646, and MCI users can obtain Call USA code numbers by calling 800-950-5555, however these services are only available to Sprint or MCI calling card holders. AT&T's similar service, USA Direct, is available to AT&T

calling card holders, as well as non-AT&T customers assuming the caller you are attempting to reach will accept collect charges. For information on AT&T's USA Direct, call 800-874-4000. (See Appendix for AT&T's country specific access codes to English-speaking operators.)

• If you are planning on driving while overseas, know the international traffic signs and rules of the road. Determine from the car rental agency whether you need an International Driver's Permit. Before you leave, ask your insurance agent about coverage in the country you are visiting. Your auto insurance may not be valid in all countries, however your credit card company may provide coverage on international car rentals purchased with your card.

• Hotel safes in foreign countries may not be as secure as in the United States. Consult your guide books, but be aware that passports, jewelry, credit card numbers and other valuables have been stolen from foreign hotel safes.

Road Tip
*Americans in a financial emergency overseas who need money fast can get help from the **Office of Overseas Citizens Services** at the Department of State. For a fee of $15 to $40, funds can be forwarded (by Western Union, bank wire, overnight delivery or mail) from a person in the U.S. to a trust account in your name at the nearest consulate or embassy. Funds can be charged to a major credit card, cashiers check, or money order. **Overseas Citizens Services** is located at CA/OCS/EMR, Room 4800, Department of State, 2201 C Street NW, Washington, D.C. 20520, (202) 647-5225.*

• American Express offers a comprehensive program to card members (and sometimes friends and relatives of card members, assuming the card member is willing to pay any fees for service) called **Global Assist**. Global Assist offers a variety of emergency medical, legal, and financial assistance through a 24-hour hotline staffed with multi-lingual operators. Beyond such pre-trip services like worldwide weather reports, passport/visa/inoculation requirements, State Department advisories, and currency exchange rates, the program offers these emergency mid-trip services:

Medical:

• Replacement of lost or stolen medications

• Referrals to English-speaking physicians, hospitals, and clinics

• Advancement of funds to pay for medical emergencies

• Medical evacuations, if necessary

Legal:

• Advancement of funds for bail or legal assistance

• Attorney referrals

Other Services:

• Relaying of messages to friends and family

• Interpreters

• Dispatchment of lost or stolen items that are found after you have departed.

The American Express Global Assist 24-hour hotline telephone number is (800) 333-2639. Outside of the United States, you can access the hotline by calling collect (202) 333-2639 or (202) 504-2639. To apply for an American

Express card and thereby become eligible for Global Assist, call (800) 528-4800.

• Scams in foreign countries can be particularly creative and elaborate. Be alert, and use your good judgment. Does a situation appear odd, or too good to be true? It probably is.

Road Tip

A seasoned traveler was the victim of a complicated scam in Italy. Unbeknownst to him, someone spilled a jar of chocolate syrup down the back of his jacket at the Milan airport. When he noticed the mess, he promptly removed his jacket to attempt to clean it off. Soon two Italian men arrived, and "sympathizing" with him, offered some tissues from their pocket and "helped" by holding up the jacket while the traveler cleaned it off. Since they only had a few tissues, they offered to go pick up some more. After the men had been gone five minutes or so, it occurred to the traveler to check his jacket pockets, and you guessed it, his passport and wallet had left with the Italian men.

Road Tip

A businessman walking through a marketplace in Oran, Algeria was surprised when two 8-year-old boys began a fist fight, right in front of him. Soon more boys joined in, and a full-fledged brawl erupted around the man. "These kids just don't seem to have put their hearts into these punches," mused the businessman, just as one of the "fighters" reached into the man's back pocket in an attempt to steal his wallet.

Passports/Visas

• Check with the embassy or consulate of the country you are visiting to determine visa requirements. You may need to obtain a work visa, assuming your trip is for business purposes.

• Photocopy your passport, and keep it with your belongings, separate from the original. In addition, leave one photocopy of your passport at home, with a family member or friend.

• Memorize your passport number. It's easy and helpful in case your passport is lost or stolen.

• While in transit, avoid holding your passport in your outer breast pocket or in your hand, where others can easily see it. This is especially true for Americans, who should avoid giving outward clues of their citizenship in certain parts of the world.

• If you feel the stamps from the countries in your passport might elicit a negative reaction, consider getting a new passport. Renewing your passport will eliminate information that might displease a terrorist.

• In the unlikely event of a hijacking, some Americans carry pseudonym passports, which are authentic-looking fake "passports" that purport your home nation to be Saint Kitts, Andorra, or some other small, neutral country. If a hijacker asks for your passport, you can offer the fake and possibly be in less danger than an American citizen. These false "passports" are advertised in most English-language international newspapers.

Safe Eating

Eating new and different foods in a foreign country is one of the most interesting things about international travel. Don't be afraid to try new things; just use the following *Road Tip* as a guide:

Road Tip: The Three P's

*You generally can feel safe eating foods in a foreign country by checking to see if the food falls into one of these categories: **P**eeled, **P**oached, or **P**iping hot. Fruits and vegetables that are peeled, rather than washed in local tap water, are usually safe. Preparing food by poaching or other boiling methods usually kills any bacteria that cause stomach problems. Similarly, most piping hot food (with steam coming off it) has been heated enough to destroy harmful bacteria.*

• Stick to bottled water (even for brushing your teeth) in countries where you are unsure about the tap water. Even on trains and airplanes, you should drink only bottled water.

• Watch out for ice, which is usually not boiled before it is frozen.

• Refer to travel guide books for the country you are visiting for complete food and drink guidelines.

Political and Other Foreign Emergencies

• Know the location of the American Consulate or Embassy in the area to which you are traveling. Americans can register their passport numbers with U.S. consulates so that in the event of a foreign emergency, the U.S. government can keep track of your whereabouts and, if necessary, assist you in exiting the country.

Road Tip

A State Department employee suggests that U.S. citizens in foreign countries can contact embassy personnel in the Consular Sections of American embassies for information on safe travel in that particular region. Don't be daunted by the long line you will probably confront at the Consular Section; most likely it's composed of non-Americans applying for visas, and U.S. citizens can go to the front, if there is not already a separate (and usually shorter) line for them.

• Check with the State Department for strategies on what to do in the event of a political emergency in the country in which you are conducting business. Strategies will vary from country to country. The following road tip illustrates the kind of nuts and bolts information that can be useful to you, and how the safe business traveler thinks.

Road Tip

A Belgian woman suggests that in the event of civil unrest or revolution, you should fill the bathtub with water, because drinking water sources are usually turned off during civil emergencies.

Useful Numbers

• **Department of State Travel Advisory**, 202-647-5225. For information on countries with dangerous or potentially dangerous travel climates for Americans.

• **Center for Disease Control (CDC), International Traveler's Hotline**, 404-332-4559, fax 404-332-4565. For information on required and recommended inoculations for foreign travel.

• **U.S. Department of Transportation, Office of Consumer Affairs**, 202-293-9142.

11

More
Useful
Numbers

The following organizations are good resources for more information about business travel.

- **American Automobile Association**
  8111 Gatehouse Road
  Falls Church, VA 22047
  800-765-4222

- **American Bed & Breakfast Association**
  10800 Midlothian Turnpike, Suite 254
  Richmond, VA 23235
  804-379-2222

- **American Hotel and Motel Association**
  1201 New York Avenue NW
  Washington, D.C. 20005-3917
  202-289-3138

- **American Society of Travel Agents**
  1101 King Street
  Alexandria, VA 22314
  703-739-2782

- **Association of Corporate Travel Executives (ACTE)**
  570 Springfield Avenue
  Summit, New Jersey 07901
  800-ACTE NOW

- **National Business Travelers' Association (NBTA)**
  177 Parsippany
  Parsippany, NJ 07054
  201-887-1552

- **National Crime Prevention Council**
  1700 K Street, N.W., Second Floor
  Washington, D.C. 20006
  202-466-6272

- **National Safety Council**
  1121 Spring Lake Drive
  Itasca, IL 60143
  708-285-1121

Appendix

AT&T International Access Numbers for English-Speaking Operators

(When a "•" appears in the Access Number, await a second dial tone before continuing. Access Numbers may not be available from every area and/or every phone.)

American Samoa 633-2-USA

Andorra .... 19 • -0011

Anguilla 1-800-872-2881

Antigua (Public Card Phones) .... #1

Argentina 001-800-200-1111

Armenia 8 0 14111

Australia 0014-881-011

Austria 022-903-011

Bahamas 1-800-872-2881

Bahrain 800-001

Belgium 078-11-0010

Belize 555

Bermuda 1-800-872-2881

Bolivia	0-800-1111
Brazil	000-8010
British Virgin Islands	1-800-872-2881
Bulgaria	00-1800-0010
Cambodia	800-0011
Cape Verde Islands	112
Cayman Islands	1-800-872-2881
Chile	00 • -0312
China, PRC	10811
Colombia	980-11-0010
Cook Islands	09-111
Costa Rica	114
Croatia	99-38-0011
Cuba (Guantanamo Bay)	935
Cyprus	080-90010
Czech Republic	00-420-00101
Denmark	8001-0010
Dominica	1-800-872-2881
Dominican Republic	1-800-872-2881
Ecuador	119
Egypt (Cairo)	510-0200
(Outside Cairo)	02-510-0200
El Salvador	190

Finland	9800-100-10
France	19 • -0011
Gabon	00 • -001
Gambia	00111
Germany	0130-0010
Ghana	0191
Gibraltar	8800
Greece	00-800-1311
Grenada	872
Guam	018-872
Guatemala	190
Guyana	165
Haiti	001-800-972-2883
Honduras	123
Hong Kong	800-1111
Hungary	00 • -800-01111
Iceland	999-001
India	000-117
Indonesia	00-801-10
Ireland	1-800-550-000
Israel	177-100-2727
Italy	172-1011
Ivory Coast	00-111-11

Jamaica	0-800-872-2881
Japan	0039-111
Kenya	0800-10
Korea	009-11
(from public phones)	11
(from U.S. Military bases)	550-HOME
Kuwait	800-288
Lebanon (Beirut)	426-801
(Outside Beirut)	01-426-801
Liberia	797-797
Liechtenstein	155-00-11
Lithuania	8 • 196
Luxembourg	0-800-0111
Macao	0800-111
Malawi	101-1992
Malaysia	800-0011
Malta	0800-890-110
Mexico	95-800-462-4240
Monaco	19 • -0011
Montserrat	1-800-872-2881
Netherlands	06 • -022-9111
Netherland Antilles	001-800-872-2881
New Zealand	000-911

Nicaragua (Managua) 174

(Outside Managua)................................. 02-174

Norway 050-12011

Panama.. 109

(from U.S. Military bases) 281-0109

Paraguay 0081-800

Peru 191

Philippines 105-11

Poland .... 0 • 010-480-0111

Portugal 05017-1-288

Romania 01-800-4288

Russia (Moscow)..................................... 155-5042

St. Kitts/Nevis.. 1-800-872-2881

Saipan.. 235-2872

San Marino 172-1011

Saudi Arabia 1-800-100

Singapore... 800-0111-111

Sierra Leone... 1100

Slovakia 00-420-00101

Spain... 900-99-00-11

Sri Lanka.. 430-430

Suriname 156

Sweden 020-795-611

Switzerland	155-00-11
Taiwan	0080-10288-0
Thailand	0019-991-1111
Turkey	9 • 9-8001-2277
Ukraine	000 • 911
United Arab Emirates	800-121
United Kingdom	0800-89-0011
Uruguay	00-0410
Venezuela	80-011-120
Zambia	00-899
Zimbabwe	110-899

Index

NOTES

ABOUT THE AUTHOR

Stacey Ravel Abarbanel is the author of
Newcomer's Handbook for Los Angeles,
(First Books). She is a regular contributor of
articles on tourism and business travel to
Meetings California, and her articles have also
appeared in *Ad LA* and *Westways.*

READER RESPONSE FORM

We welcome comments regarding *Smart Business Travel: How to Stay Safe When You're On the Road.* If you have suggestions or have found any mistakes and omissions, or, if you would just like to express your opinion about the guide, please let us know! We will consider any comments and give respondents a 25% discount off a second edition. Please send this response form to:

First Books, Inc.
P.O. Box 578147
Chicago, IL 60657

Comments: _____

_____

_____

_____

_____

_____

_____

_____

_____

_____

_____

Name _____

Address _____

City _____ State _____ Zip _____

SAFE BUSINESS TRAVEL SEMINARS:

Make sure your employees know How to Stay Safe When They're On the Road

- Are the employees at your company taking every precaution they can to ensure their safety on business trips?

- Do they check the identity of hotel employees, before they allow them into their rooms?

- Do they ensure that the car they get into at the airport is truly a certified taxi?

- Are they careful to remove their name tags once their meetings are over and they are out on the street?

These are just a few of the many tips offered during **Safe Business Travel Seminars** led by Stacey Ravel Abarbanel, author of *Smart Business Travel*. Abarbanel has surveyed safety experts and long-time business travelers to compile an inventory of no-nonsense ideas on how to be safer on business trips. Your company's employees will come away from the seminar not scared, but better prepared for the many eventualities that can befall them during their business travels.

For more information about hands-on business travel seminars geared to the needs of your company, contact:

Jeremy Solomon
First Books Seminars
(312) 276-5911
Fax (312) 276-5977

FIT TO TRAVEL:

How to Stay Fit When You're On the Road

	#/Copies		Total
Fit to Travel	_____	x $12.95	$_____
Tax (IL residents add 8.75% sales tax)			$_____
Postage & Handling ($6.00 first book, $.75 each add'l)			$_____
		Total	$_____

Ship To:

Name_____

Title_____

Company_____

Address_____

City_____ State_____ Zip_____

Phone Number _____

Send this order form and a check or money order
payable to First Books, Inc.

First Books, Inc. Mail Order Department
P.O. Box 578147, Chicago, IL 60657
(312) 276-5911

Allow 2-4 weeks for delivery.

NEWCOMER'S HANDBOOKS™

Are you moving (or thinking of moving) to New York City, Chicago, Los Angeles, Washington D.C. or Boston? If so, our guides to these cities–written for newcomers (not tourists)–are the perfect introduction.

	#/Copies		Total
NewComer's Boston	_____	x $13.95	$_____
NewComer's Chicago	_____	x $12.00	$_____
NewComer's Los Angeles	_____	x $12.95	$_____
NewComer's New York City	_____	x $15.95	$_____
NewComer's Washington, DC	_____	x $13.95	$_____
		Subtotal	$_____
	Tax (IL residents add 8.75% sales tax)		$_____
	Postage & Handling ($6.00 first book, $.75 each add'l)		$_____
		Total	$_____

Ship To:

Name_____

Title_____

Company_____

Address_____

City_____ State_____ Zip_____

Phone Number _____

Send this order form and a check or money order
payable to First Books, Inc.
First Books, Inc. Mail Order Department
P.O. Box 578147, Chicago, IL 60657, (312) 276-5911
Allow 2-4 weeks for delivery.